Angel in Disguise

by Violeta Barrett

Designed by Flavia Harvey

SPIDER BOOKS
PUBLISHING

Angel in Disguise

Children's Edition
Published by Spider Books Publishing
Printed by CreateSpace
Copyright 2014 Violeta Barrett

ISBN-10: 1497316901
ISBN-13: 9781497316904

*Dedicated to
my beloved
Butzi*

Chapter 1

I t was not love at first sight when Violeta initially saw him. In fact, she had an aversion to cats and always assumed that she was a dog person, having owned three different breeds of dogs over the course of her married life. So when the sound came again, a sort of scratching noise, she responded with some annoyance when she saw a cat, stretched to his full height, clawing the screen door to her summer kitchen.

"Cut that out!" she scolded without realizing the pun. She didn't need one more repair bill. Gently he lowered himself and then circled the small porch of Violeta's country home before approaching the screen again.

"No!" she said emphatically. She reached for a newspaper, rolled it into a tube, and opened the door latch. He backed off but didn't seem too intimidated. Stretching out horizontally on his back in front of the door, he matched Violeta eyeball to eyeball. Violeta pushed the door open slightly, and he got up to move his position, watching her with interest as she came out. He was not frightened away, even when she dragged the porch rocker over to sit down. Intrepid little fellow! It was obvious that she was no threat to him, paper or no paper. Suddenly he rolled over on his back again, half this way, half that way, his head in an upside down position.

"Is that how cats behave?" she thought. "Cute!"

Violeta leaned her head against the high-backed chair, rocking gently. Her eyes took in the beauty that surrounded her. A red-breasted robin picked away at a worm in the green lawn and then flew to a nest hidden in the lilac bushes. The tall maple trees filtered the rays of the early morning sun. A breeze played among the branches so that they parted, allowing a sunbeam to alight upon this small, furry creature of the wild; he must have been untamed, judging from the nips on his right ear and left eyelid. Yet Violeta

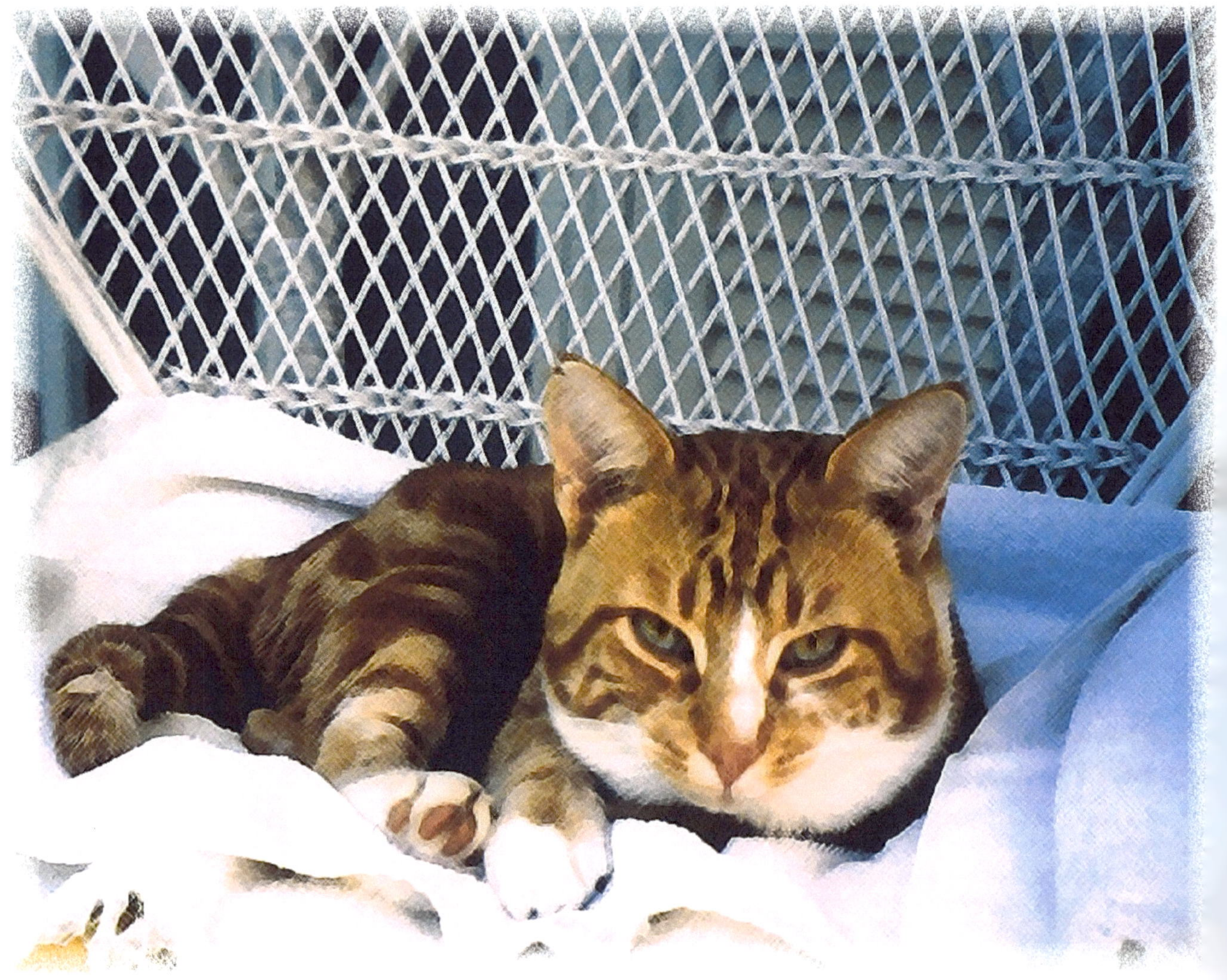

couldn't help but notice how beautiful he was in spite of his injuries: his fur was almost the shade of autumn leaves with white markings on his chest and paws, on the side of his nose, and circling his tail. His eyes, when the sunlight caught them, appeared translucent, in a delicate shade of aquamarine.

Well now, what next? She *could* give him some milk and water…that would do…then he'd probably get bored and leave. Done! He lapped it up thirstily. But instead of leaving, he stalked across the porch to the other rocker, curled up on it, and, with a shake of his tail and one final look at Violeta, closed his eyes.

"So, *that's* a catnap," Violeta thought in amusement. "Well, at least it will help pass the time…for both of us." She rocked and he napped. And, for the moment, at least, it seemed that a sense of normalcy had returned to Violeta's life.

It had been nearly two years since her husband passed away; the worst nightmare she could ever imagine had still not ended. Coming to terms with her loss—the emptiness, the aloneness—had taken a heavy toll on her. The house that they had lovingly built together, nestled on a hill in picturesque Northumberland County, Ontario, now seemed far too big for one person.

She looked over at the cat. The soft contours of his body rose and fell with his breathing, reminding her of ripples on a pond. His nose twitched ever so often.

Was he dreaming or was it just an itch? So at peace. What wouldn't she give to sleep like that. She sighed faintly.

Well, she had better things to do than just sit there watching a cat sleep. Puttering about the house, she realized by late afternoon that she hadn't eaten anything since breakfast. When she reentered the kitchen, she was reminded of her visitor who, it was apparent, had left.

The following morning, she staggered down to breakfast after another restless night. As she prepared the coffee, the constant movement of a shadow crossing the stream of sunlight on the kitchen floor caught her attention. Again. And still again. She glanced out the picture window. There, on the chair that he'd occupied the previous day, sat the cat, rocking to and fro. Upon seeing her face in the window, he jumped to the porch floor and began to scratch at the screen door. Not again! But somehow, she was in a better mood than she was the day before. His presence gave her a warm, comfy feeling. He had come back, and she liked it!

Most days he returned, and she could see a pattern developing. Other times, when he didn't show up–the hunter's instinct being a stronger pull than the attention he received from her–she felt a pang of sadness. She reprimanded herself for letting him reach her soft spot. Violeta wanted no attachments. Never again. No, not even a pet.

However, there was no harm in putting two dishes for food and water on a plastic mat on the porch. It was the humane thing to do, after all. And the old puppy collar that she put on him with a note containing her telephone number was just in case he belonged to someone. But no one called, and he kept coming back.

2

Chapter

As the summer wore on, Violeta realized that a chink had opened in her heart. Smiles that had become so rare over the past two years began to emerge from their hiding place. She found herself looking forward to each new day because of this tiny presence that had come from nowhere into her life.

Days when she gardened, he'd be there beside her, or nearby, sometimes purring his approval, sometimes dashing up a tree to show her his versatility. Other times, he would *hide* in the bushes, calling for her to *seek* him. Or he would chase after a cloud of butterflies dancing past or pursue a pair of humming birds fluttering round her feeder. She cherished most the times when she returned from a day of shopping and found him waiting for her to return, still curled up on the rocker that had become his, exactly as she had left him.

The relationship between them had begun to flourish.

One day they entered new territory in their ability to communcate. "Cat," that's what she called him (no attachments, remember?), began to get restless, the signal that he was preparing to head off for the woods and fields that surrounded her home. Violeta thought of *The Call of the Wild*, so appropriately named by Jack London. Cat started for the road, looking back once or twice, pausing to rest on the pebbled driveway, each time moving further away from the house. Then with a loud "MEOW" in her direction, he ducked under the wooden fence and began his leisurely gait up the road. She watched him from the porch, feeling the loneliness creep back.

"Meow! MEOW!" This time it wasn't Cat. It was Violeta! He turned to look, and then he responded with his own "Meow." She replied and he answered again. What seemed so natural to him was uncanny to Violeta. Even after he disappeared from view, they kept it up. It was all she could do to refrain from running after him and enveloping him in her arms, for surely this tiny ball of fur was heaven-sent.

Tears spilled from the corners of her eyes and down her cheeks as she turned away. She sat on the porch step for a while, her face in her hands, trying to compose herself. "I'm having a bad day," she thought. "I promised myself 'never again,' and here I am, crying like a baby over a silly cat." Another burst of fresh tears pushed their way down her face. Suddenly she felt a tickle on her cheek followed by a strange roughness, like wet sandpaper. It was Cat's whiskers, and then his tiny pink tongue. He had returned.

Chapter 3

August was the hottest month that year in Ontario. And it was the only time when Violeta could enjoy a swim in Lake Ontario, where the temperature of the water almost year round was generally too cold. She decided to take Cat with her. The drive to Cobourg Beach was only a half hour away.

Carrying her beach chair, a large tote bag, *and* Cat, she stepped lightly onto the hot sand. She found a quiet spot not too far from the lake but close enough to the park for a shady walk if she or Cat felt up to it. The children's play area was a short distance away, and she could hear the joyful screams of little tots as they ran back and forth tirelessly under the large sprinkler system.

Violeta spread out a thin cotton throw and set Cat on it. His eyes were nearly popping out of his head with curiosity and fear. This must have been unexplored territory for him, and Violeta could tell that he wasn't sure he liked it. Still wearing the puppy collar and leash of his predecessor, which Violeta had looped around the chair leg, he sat as still as a sphinx, barely moving a muscle. "What is this strange place and what is that huge body of water directly ahead?" he seemed to be thinking. Cat apparently had never seen anything like it before, especially the white-capped waves rolling in, splashing gently on the shore.

Most cats have an aversion to water and Cat was no exception. So when Violeta undid the leash from the chair and began to walk toward the shoreline, Cat pulled back.

"Come closer!" urged Violeta, not realizing that Cat would not approach the lake and would prefer to be as far from it as possible.

Unthinking, Violeta picked Cat up and started to walk into the refreshing, cool water. Cat wriggled and squirmed, freeing himself from her grasp. He ran to the dry sand, looking left and right, unsure what to do. Violeta followed as quickly as she could, stomping on the wet leash that dragged behind Cat, stopping him in his tracks in the nick of time. Grabbing his collar, she picked him up and walked back to their space. Cat's body was shaking with fright; his wet fur stood on end. She knotted the leash around the leg of the chair again and set him down in it, facing away from the lake so that he could see the trees in the park instead. Kneeling on the throw, Violeta rubbed him dry with a beach towel as she spoke to him soothingly, petting his back and head until he calmed down. Reaching into the tote bag, she took out his stuffed mouse and laid it next to him. He glanced at it, and then stretched out his pink-padded paw to touch it. Soon he had it in his mouth, content to play with his familiar toy.

"Well, that was dumb!" Violeta exclaimed aloud. "Sorry, Cat. I should have known that cats and water don't mix." Cat looked into Violeta's eyes as if he could understand her. Apology accepted. He returned his attention to his stuffed mouse.

By now, the sun was beating down on them. "Why didn't I bring the beach umbrella?" Violeta thought. Cat had a better plan.

The chair, which was a short-legged type, had just enough room under the seat for Cat to fit. Slowly he stepped down onto the throw and squeezed

his body into the shaded area beneath the seat.

"Leave room for me!" laughed Violeta, marveling at Cat's ingenuity. Tying the towel ends to the backrest of the chair, Violeta pulled the towel over her head, improvising a temporary tent. She took out her thermos of cold water and poured some in the cap for Cat, who lapped it up in seconds. Violeta drank directly from the thermos. Well, she wasn't going to get her swim today, it seemed. But they'd sit a while longer, postpone the practice walk through the park for another time, and soon head home. Cat had experienced enough trauma for one day. He appeared calm and content now, and that was what mattered. He looked at her, tilting his head to the side.

"I know what you're thinking," Violeta said, noticing Cat's telling look. "Whoever said 'Life's a Beach' was certainly not a cat!"

4

Chapter

The summer passed, and soon the leaves turned golden brown, and red and bright yellow. The countryside was a mosaic of fall colors. Fields were covered with orange pumpkins and evenly patterned with bales of hay. Violeta's thoughts began to turn to other things. She would be leaving soon for the warmer climate of Florida, where she spent the winter. What would become of Cat?

Advice came freely from everyone she knew. From the farmers, "Don't worry about him. He can fend for himself." From the neighbors, "Surely you aren't considering taking him with you, my dear. Do you really need any more problems right now?" From friends, "How can you leave him behind?" A visit to the veterinarian was in order.

"You know, cats are very adaptable," the veterinarian said. Adaptable! The key word. With a little more than a month to go, Violeta had a lot of soul-searching to do. First of all, was she doing the right thing by Cat or was she only thinking of herself?

The vet was her ally. "Get him inoculated. No harm in that. I'll give him a checkup and a good bath. And after a few days, see how you feel about it. I would also recommend cutting his front nails but not the back ones. And I definitely would not declaw him. That's too painful. And besides, should you decide it doesn't work, he needs those nails for his own protection. Remember, the decision is entirely up to you."

Yes, it was. But Violeta had a lot of work ahead of her if she intended to go through with this well-intentioned idea. She agreed to the shots, the bath, the nail cutting, and the checkup. At least now she was assured that Cat was in good health and free of fleas. But he hadn't been indoors yet and needed to be housebroken. She convinced herself that this too would not hamper him if she decided not to follow through with her plan.

After purchasing a litter box, a bag of litter, and a scooper, she began the training. Her first attempts were a disaster. She did all the right things; he did all the wrong ones…or was it the other way around? To begin with, she spread newspaper in the center of the tile bathroom floor. Next, she placed the litter box on top, then removed the cover. She picked up Cat and placed him in the box. She put the lid of the toilet seat down and sat there watching Cat. Cat, in turn, watched her. "Was this some new game they were playing?" his expression seemed to say. After a while, Cat appeared bored, climbed out of the box and sat down on the paper. Violeta, got up and placed him back in the box. They continued to stare at each other.

"If I were his mother, I could teach him what to do," she thought. "It's not as easy as I thought it would be. I'll try leaving the room and see what happens."

She did, returning after a short while. Cat was pacing the floor. Violeta decided to move the box to the side wall. She placed the lid back on top of the box. Frustrated, she returned to her seat to continue her watch.

Just when she was about to declare defeat, she stared in amazement as he stepped carefully into the covered box.

Digging a hole in the litter, he turned to face forward, then squatted. It was as though he knew how all the time and was simply testing her patience.

When he was through, he worked up a storm covering it, then stepped from the box and eyed her. Clearly the look said, "What's a guy gotta do for some privacy?"

Whooping for joy, Violeta lifted him high and danced him around the room. Mission accomplished! On to the next challenge.

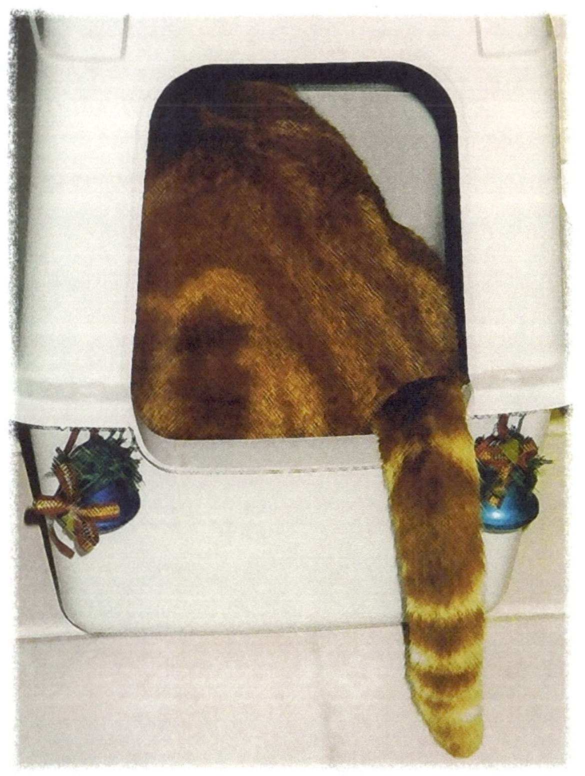

5

Chapter

The morning brought another lovely fall day, so Violeta decided the time had come to start training Cat to walk properly on a leash. His new royal blue cat collar, which matched the leash, had a tiny silver bell that tingled as he ambled along the side of the road. Cat was about to learn another lesson in what it means to be domesticated.

As they walked along, the gravel crunched under Violeta's steps, but she scarcely heard a sound coming from Cat. At first he walked so quietly beside her that she couldn't tell sometimes whether he was there unless he touched her pant leg. She was fascinated by his graceful gait and the awe he expressed at what he saw in his world. He stopped often to smell a wild mint leaf or extend a paw to something lying on the side of the road. Violeta dared not imagine what he thought it was. He would lift his tiny pink nose to whiff at a breeze. Sometimes he would sit and watch a withered leaf slowly make its descent to the ground. Then he'd gently touch it to hear it crackle. He would pull at a blade of grass and chew off a piece. Over and over he would roll in the moist earth and stones. Every rut in the road was a stopping point to lap with gusto the rain that hadn't yet seeped into the earth. Every drop of morning dew that filled a fallen leaf seemed to him to taste like nectar from the gods.

Soon it appeared that he became accustomed to the leash, and he pulled away until he felt the hold it had. He gave Violeta one of his looks, and she soon found that he was taking *her* for a walk as she followed his lead. They walked for about a mile, stopping to examine things she had never noticed before. Passing the beaver pond, she was glad there were no signs of any beavers, for by now she knew that Cat would not hesitate to go after anything that moved, pulling her along with him.

A flurry of wings told Violeta they had disturbed a group of grouse hidden in a pile of leaves that almost matched their reddish-brown color. She held tight to Cat's leash as he tried to chase them.

The sun had hidden behind a large, gray cloud. Violeta looked up at the sky and noticed that the weather had turned. Time to head back before they got caught in a rain shower. She tugged at the leash, but Cat had no intention of turning back. Stubbornly, he lay down as though preparing to play a game of tug-of-war. Violeta felt a rain drop. This was no time for play. She bent to pick up Cat. He struggled for a while, but Violeta won the battle. She had a few scratches to prove it. Running most of the way, she reached the porch seconds before the clouds burst.

The following morning, when she was brushing Cat, Violeta noticed that the tiny bell on his collar was missing. "Oh no," she thought. "I loved that little bell. It probably came off during our pulling match." She pouted momentarily and then tried to put it out of her mind. It could so easily be replaced. Not like other lost things. Still...

The next day the sun shone brightly again, inviting another walk. The road was still soggy from the heavy rain; the pale gray-and-white gravel was dark, almost the color of yesterday's cloud-covered sky. Progress was slow, as Cat, now used to the leash, stopped every few minutes to lie on the wet leaves or grass. Violeta, who had become more observant, noticed the wild grapes and raspberries still on the vines and bushes, and the marvelous abundance of tall grasses and fall plants.

"It's glorious to think how Mother Earth sprouts forth this life year after year," she thought. This time, she also spied some interesting stone specimens along the road. She bent to select a few of the more colorful ones, much like walking along a beach and picking up a shell here and there. Even at a leisurely pace, they had traveled some distance when suddenly Cat lay down on the gravel. Violeta tugged on the leash, but Cat remained firm. He moved slightly to the side, and Violeta noticed the shiny, round-shaped object half-hidden by his furry belly.

"It couldn't be! What are the chances?" she thought. But it was. Cat's silver bell.

6
Chapter

To get Cat used to long-distance driving, Violeta bought an inexpensive cardboard pet carrier. Either it was too small or he was too big, but when she looked over at him, scrunched inside that crate on the front passenger seat, there was no question that she had to chuck out that idea. So instead, she strapped him into a harness leash, which she laced through a hook on the roof of her convertible, allowing enough room for him to sit or lie down on his pillow. This arrangement worked for a while, until he discovered that he had enough lead to cross over to her lap. That suited him fine, but Violeta believed in safety first. A cat in your lap while driving was a no-no. So a large piece of cardboard slipped between the front seats, just low enough for him to see over, did the trick.

Daily they drove through the countryside. At first Cat let her know with a loud, lamenting meow that he was very displeased with her control over his freedom. But as the scenes flashed past his window in rapid succession, they left him "speechless" with wonder, and he gradually complained less and less. Each time they ventured out, he would eventually tire of the moving pictures, and with a wide yawn, followed by another, his eyelids would close as he fell fast asleep.

7

Chapter

Violeta started to let Cat indoors. Now that he was housebroken, Violeta decided he would be nice company at the foot of her bed instead of on the cat bed in the kitchen. Besides, it was a king-sized bed with lots of room to spare.

She coaxed him away from the large, empty paper bag he loved crawling into. It always made her chuckle, as it was obvious that he thought he was completely hidden from sight, unaware that his butt and long tail were still exposed.

She climbed the stairs to her bedroom, placing the litter box on the tile floor of the adjoining bathroom. Once she got into bed, Cat quickly followed. This was the lap of luxury, he must have

thought, as he rolled over on the soft, thick comforter. From the bed, Violeta watched TV for a while, glancing over at Cat every few minutes to see his reaction. Much to her surprise, he wasn't the least bit interested in it, and she wondered whether he even saw the picture on the tube.

When she finally tired, Violeta shut off the TV, and with one last stroke of Cat's soft, silky head, she rolled over to turn off the light. Cat purred contentedly while Violeta exhaled a long, deep breath.

A short time passed. Violeta was not yet asleep when she felt a movement on the bed. It was hard to see in the dark, but she knew Cat had jumped off. "I wonder why?" she thought. "He certainly seemed to like it here." An idea entered her head… or was it intuition?

She reached for the lamp switch just as she felt a thump on the mattress. As the light went on, Cat appeared at the foot of the bed. Even without looking she sensed what she would see, and with a scream and a leap, she was out of the bed lickety-split. Down the stairs she ran, springing onto a dining room chair. In a second she was crouched on top of the table, squealing and shrieking at the top of her lungs. She shuddered in disgust, trying to compose herself.

Anyone who has lived in the country knows that field mice are a part of country life. So when the weather turns cold, they seek warmer shelter and are bound to come indoors.

Violeta finally calmed down. She began to have misgivings. Could she have imagined it? She tried to convince herself that she was mistaken.

Sitting on the table with her legs tucked under her, she forced herself to think clearly. However, she didn't have long to wait. Facing the stairs, she spotted Cat slowly descending. First her focus was on him, but she quickly noticed something else the moment he stepped to the tile entry floor. In his mouth, held high with pride, wriggled a tiny brown form with a tail. Spying her on the table, Cat approached her with his gift.

Violeta was up and running. She sprinted to the top of the stairs in seconds, slamming shut the bedroom door.

Chapter 8

She scarcely remembered whether she had had a moment's sleep, but when she removed the covers from her head, the light was streaming in from the French door to her tiny Juliet balcony. She lay there a while, thinking. If only her husband were still alive, he would have laughed at her antics and taken care of the intruder. Now there was no one she could call.

Violeta grabbed her robe and bravely opened the bedroom door. Cat was not there. She cautiously descended the steps. As she reached the bottom, she looked around. There, under the dining room table, sat Cat. He was not alone. He didn't notice her as he playfully flipped the tiny dead corpse in the air, from one paw to the other.

Violeta sprang into action. She ran outside to the garage and grabbed the shovel with the longest handle and then headed back to the house. As she opened the front door as wide as it would go, she let out a yell. Cat dropped his prey. Violeta scooped it up in one swoop and ran out the door, down the stone steps, across the grass, through the open wooden gate, and to the other side of the road.

She swung around and hurled the contents of the shovel into the woods as far as it could go, all the while screaming at the top of her lungs. Cat watched from the doorway, totally perplexed. Clearly, his expression said, "Don't look a gift horse in the mouth."

Chapter 9

In southern Ontario, one of the surest signs of fall, besides the changing colors of foliage, is the sight of skeins of Canada geese flying across the sky in a *V* formation on their way to their winter home in the southern United States or Mexico. Violeta heard their telltale honking and ran to the bedroom balcony where she could get a clear view. This annual event evoked deep-seated emotions in her as she stared in wonderment at this amazing phenomenon that marked the passage of time and the turning of seasons. Cat sat beside her, looking first at these flying waterfowls, and then at her with a look of curiosity. Once out of sight, the birds seemed to be out of mind, and he slinked off to his litter box to answer another of nature's calls.

"Hello! HELL-O-O! Are you in?"

It was Rita, Violeta's friend and neighbor, who was a weekend resident of a small, charming farm about a mile down the road. She always stopped for a visit, usually bringing some homemade meal or dessert. She worried that Violeta, who had lost so much weight, was not eating properly.

"Here I am!" Violeta called out from the top of the stairs. She raced down the steps, turning the corner from the sunken living room into the country kitchen, two steps up. "I was hoping you would visit. Would you like some tea?" She unlatched the screen door and hugged her friend. As usual, Rita put a covered dish on the counter. "Your supper," she said. Violeta thanked her before filling the kettle.

"Tea will just hit the spot," answered Rita. "We've had a busy day harvesting. Say, where's Cat?"

"At the moment, he's indisposed. But he'll be here shortly. You can bet on that. After all, think of the power he has over you." Violeta always tried to put on a happy face no matter what she was feeling. She'd had another restless night.

"Here's a box of Kleenex," she said. "You'd better be prepared."

Rita suffered from allergies, and cat dander especially bothered her. But it didn't keep her away. Whenever she stopped in, she'd have a tearing session for most of the visit.

At that moment, like a ballet dancer, Cat leaped into the kitchen and headed directly toward Rita, recognizing her at once. He brushed up against her leg. Rita bent down to pet him. "Hi, Cat!" she said. "Boy, he's getting fat. You must be feeding him well. Wonder what he ate before taking up residence with you?"

"Let's not go into that. What a night!" Violeta told her about the field mouse episode, and Rita howled with laughter. "Get used to it. The cold weather has only just begun."

Unlike Violeta, who had been a city girl all her life, Rita wasn't, so small rodents didn't bother her. In her native Switzerland, it had been part of country life, just as it was here.

"Well, I can't stay long today, much as I'd like to. Just came by to invite you to Toronto to see our new apartment. Can you make it next Thursday?"

"I'll have to check my social calendar," Violeta joked, walking over to the hutch cabinet where she kept the calendar marked with appointments. Lawyer, financial manager, eye exam.

"Thursday is good!" she said. "You'll have to give me specific directions. I haven't been to that part of Toronto in years."

Rita wrote out instructions on a piece of paper while Violeta fixed the tea and biscuits. They sat and talked for a while. Cat lay on the indoor mat, grooming himself. He'd stop long enough to nod each time Rita let out a sneeze, as if keeping score.

"Well, I'd better be going. We want to make an early start to beat the traffic. Come about eleven so I can show you around the community as well. It'll do you good to get away from here for a change."

Thursday arrived, and the idea of an outing to visit Rita's new digs pleased Violeta; but she had been awake most of the night, so she almost declined. The alternative of staying home alone, though, forced her to get up and go, as she was beginning to experience cabin fever.

Violeta felt tense behind the wheel of the car, particularly as she approached Toronto. The twelve-lane highway traffic was heavy. Except for one small mistake of overshooting an exit, she managed to find Rita's complex. It felt like that mistake was destined to happen, though, because instead of coming from the East, she arrived from the West, and the physical environment began to look familiar.

When Violeta stopped for a red light, she looked out the passenger-side window. A sign read *Shoreline Towers*. Uncanny! This was her first apartment when she came to live in Toronto thirty-two years ago as a "landed immigrant" from Brooklyn, New York.

Landed immigrant. What an incongruous term. (Did that mean her dog Bonnie had been a landed immigrant too?) She remembered being carried over the threshold into her first home in a foreign land. Was it coincidence that Rita should live only a few doors away?

The afternoon flew by. Lunch was a delicious Scandinavian-style smorgas-bord (except that it was Swiss!) The apartment was beautiful and showed Rita's flair for decorating. The spectacular view overlooked the great expanse of Lake Ontario. Outside they walked along curving paths lined with bushes and trees. They conversed non-stop, and the hours melted away. Soon it was time to leave.

Violeta didn't feel nearly as tired as she should have—even though she arrived home after dark. As she put the key in the door, she glanced at the porch window. Cat was sitting on the sill awaiting her arrival. The house didn't feel so empty after all. The kitchen radio was playing. Strange! She

remembered shutting it off before she left. She checked. The radio switch was off. She realized she hadn't shut off the house alarm when she entered, yet it didn't give off its deafening shrill. And when she went upstairs to change her clothes, the tiny music box began to play on its own. Cat had followed her upstairs and sat on the bed watching her, following her every move. She smiled at him, telling him about her day. From across the room, he gave her a slow "eye blink," which Violeta had learned from other cat owners is considered a cat kiss. "How sweet!" she thought. Leaning forward to pet his soft fur, Violeta looked deep into Cat's eyes and blinked back.

No doubt about it. This was one enchanted day.

Chapter 10

Still uncertain that her new venture would work, Violeta kept hedging until her hand was forced. The day before she was scheduled to leave, an overnight storm dumped ten inches of snow on the ground. She opened the kitchen door to let Cat out. If he left now, she told herself, it was over. He would probably not return in time.

Out the door Cat slinked provocatively, testing the snow with his paw. One step forward, and he suddenly vanished into a snow bank. Seconds later, propelling like a rocket, he landed in the bushes that landscaped the house. Fate would have to take its course. Violeta still had so many arrangements to complete, and now there was the snow to contend with.

Most of the things she packed were already in the car. All that was left was Cat's stuff. Part of the morning she spent covering the furniture, unplugging the lamps and refrigerator, draining the pipes. She completed the necessary phone calls to the power company, the telephone company, the security company, and her close friends and neighbors. Finally, by midafternoon, she headed to the garage to shovel a path to and from the house. With any luck, the road would be plowed by morning.

Her heart felt heavier than her snow boots as she approached the front porch. No sign of Cat. Violeta paused to listen to the silence. The winter-wonderland scene was a thing of beauty. The hills were sparkling from the fresh snow, and the branches of the tall cedar trees that surrounded the house were still coated in powdery flakes in spite of the slight wind. Far off, beyond the valley, the Trent River shimmered icy blue in the sunlight.

Suddenly, from beneath the shelter of the bushes, a small copper-colored head with markings of white peeked out.

"Meow!"

The sign was unmistakable! He had been there all the time. Kneeling in the snow, she reached under the bush and lifted out her little angel. Her voice sounded strange, like she'd swallowed a bubble.

"Come on, Cat," Violeta said. "Let's get packing!"

Postscript to Parents and/or Children's Story Readers

This children's version of ANGEL IN DISGUISE was deliberately shortened from its original version to allow younger children to enjoy part of Cat and Violeta's adventure. If your child has enjoyed the story so far, then they might love to hear the rest of the story.

To order the original 148 page book, it is available at Amazon and other retail bookstores, or directly from the author's website: www.violetabarrett.com.

ISBN-13: 9781484092217